Petting Zoo

Gail Tuchman

SCHOLASTIC INC.

New York   Toronto   London   Auckland
Sydney   Mexico City   New Delhi   Hong Kong

Read more! Do more!

After you read this book, download your free all-new digital activities.

1

petting zoo

reading fun

SCHOLASTIC discover more readers

enter

For Mac and PC

ADMIT ONE 389002

You can show what a great reader you are!

Petting zoo counting

Click on the correct numbers.

click — DISCOVER MORE
home — BACK TO THE START

How many calves are there?	How many animals wallow in mud?	How many animals have webbed feet?	How many animals lay eggs?	How many animals are there in total?
4 2 3	2 7 4	7 3 8	6 8 10	16 20 18

Do quizzes about the
fun facts in this book!

Make some finger puppets!

Choose your favourite animal
from the petting zoo to make.

back — SCREEN BEFORE
home — BACK TO THE START

You will need . . .

A pencil
Thin white card

Markers, crayons, or
paints and a paintbrush

Scissors
A glue stick

Duck   Chicken   Goat   Pony   Sheep   Cow   Pig   Guinea pig   Alpaca

ow click
e numbers . . .   1   2   3   4   5

Play petting zoo games and do
activities with videos and sounds!

Log on to
www.scholastic.com/discovermore/readers
Enter this special code: **L16DTMFN4T61**

BAA! CLUCK! MOO!
The animals are calling.
They're calling to you.

GOATS

SHEEP

BUNNIES

Come and see
the animals.

PONIES

COWS

ALPACAS

DUCKS

REMEMBER TO:

Pick up a map!

Wash your hands!

PIGS

Come and feed them at the petting zoo.

CHICKENS

GUINEA PIGS

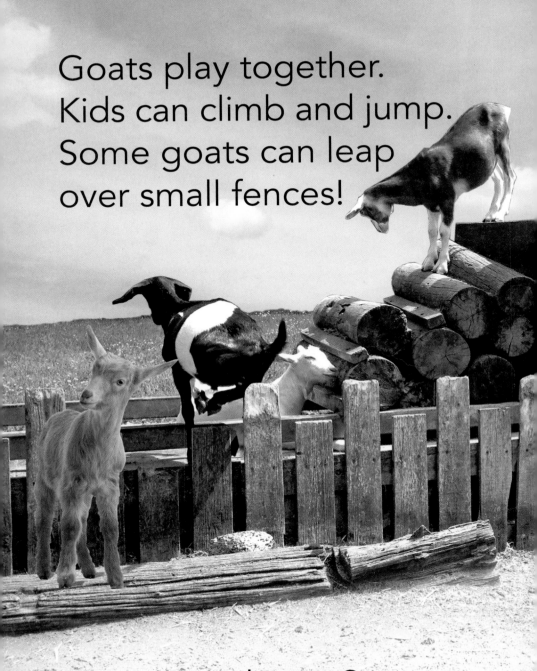

Goats play together.
Kids can climb and jump.
Some goats can leap
over small fences!

Goats are clever. Some
can even open gates.

Billy
(male
goat)

Nanny
(female
goat)

Kid
(young
goat)

Goats check out new things. They sniff and nibble them.

Hay

Good food for goats

oats plants grass maize

Maybe the new thing is food! Goats spend half their time eating.

HOLD A GOAT CAREFULLY.

9

Sheep get haircuts, like you do. A sheep's coat is called a fleece. It needs to be sheared, or cut, every spring.

NEW WORD

shear
sheer
A sheep is **sheared** once a year.

SAY IT OUT LOUD

10

Shearing doesn't hurt the sheep.

GIVE MILK TO A LAMB.

Fleece is turned into wool.

Wool

Fleece

Wool is turned into clothes.

Sweater

11

Bunnies do something called binkying.

They jump up into the air.

BRUSH A BUNNY

Then they
twist and kick
their feet.

Alpacas
hum.
Listen
closely.

They hum
softly
to one
another.

Wild alpacas live on mountains. They are in the camel family.

North America

South America

Wild alpacas live in South America.

Wild alpaca herd

An alpaca will cry out if there is danger.

TOUCH AN ALPACA'S SOFT HAIR.

15

Webbed feet work like paddles. They help ducks swim well in the water.

HOLD DUCKLINGS GENTLY.

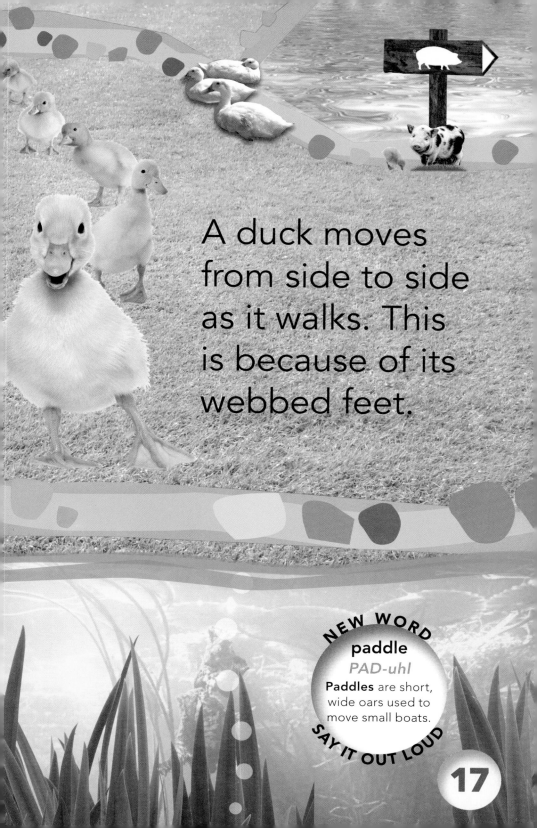

A duck moves from side to side as it walks. This is because of its webbed feet.

NEW WORD

paddle

PAD-uhl

Paddles are short, wide oars used to move small boats.

SAY IT OUT LOUD

Piglets grow fast. They weigh about 1 kilogram at birth. In 6 months, they may be 90 kilograms!

STROKE A PIGLET.

A mother pig gives milk to her piglets.

SNUGGLE A GUINEA PIG.

Guinea pigs weigh about 1 kilogram. They are not in the pig family!

Pigs can't sweat to cool down. They wallow, or roll around in wet mud.

MUD FACTOR 50

The mud helps stop sunburn. It also keeps bugs off pigs.

Animals that wallow

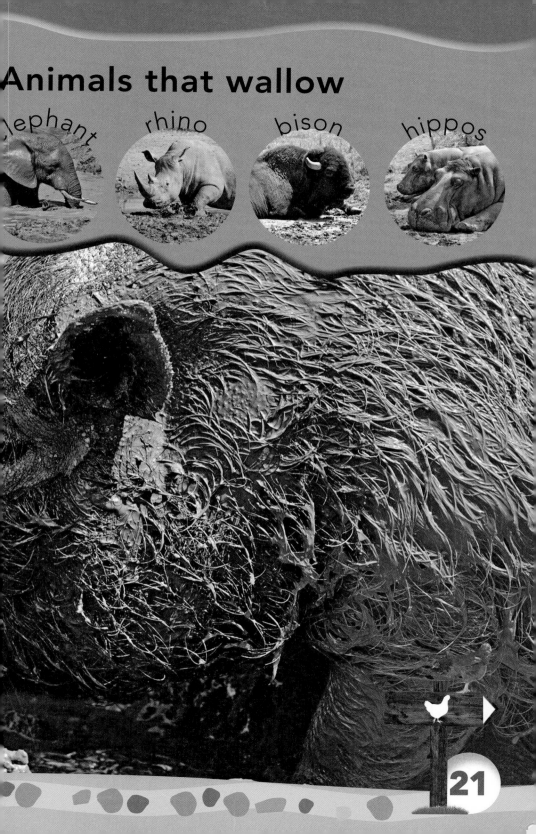

elephant

rhino

bison

hippos

A hen can lay an egg almost every day. She sits on her eggs to keep them warm. The eggs will hatch into chicks.

All birds hatch from eggs.

Quail   Robin   Chicken   Duck

Chicken

Chicks grow up to be chickens.

Chick

Egg

Hatching

Penguin

Goose

Emu

Ostrich

Chickens have combs on their heads. Combs come in lots of shapes.

Comb

FEED A CHICKEN CORN.

Types of combs

Single

Rose

24

Chickens have wattles on their heads. These keep them cool.

NEW WORD

wattle
WAH-tuhl
Turkeys can also have **wattles** on their heads.

SAY IT OUT LOUD

Wattle

Pea

V-shaped

Walnut

A baby cow is called a calf.

Calf

Cow

Dr Cathe and
Dr Nick are vets.
They helped
a calf.

Little Nicky
"The calf was very weak.
We wrapped him in our
jackets. We put him
under a heat lamp to
keep him warm. It
worked! He stood up
the next day."

Little
Nicky

Before you leave, how about a ride on this pony? Your family can take pictures.

Saddle . . . . ➤

Ponies and horses are different. Ponies are usually smaller.

What a great day at the petting zoo!

Ride a pony.

Stroke a bunny.

Hold a chick.

Say hello to a goat.

Feed a piglet.

exit

29

Glossary

comb
The colourful piece of skin on top of a chicken's head.

fleece
The soft, woolly coat of a sheep.

hatch
To be born by breaking out of an egg.

herd
A large group of animals.

nibble
To eat something by taking small bites.

shear
To cut the hair or wool off a sheep or other animal.

vet
A doctor who treats sick or hurt animals.

wallow
To roll around in mud or water.

wattle
The fold of skin under the head or neck of a chicken, turkey, or other bird.

webbed
Having toes that are connected by folds of skin.

ndex

Remember to wash your hands after touching an animal.

Disclaimer: This book is not intended for instruction. Adult supervision and best judgment should always be used when interacting with animals. Be sure to follow all rules when visiting a petting zoo.

For their generosity of time in sharing their veterinary passion and expertise, special thanks to Dr Cathe Montesano and Dr Nick Tallarico. Thank you also to the petting zoo at DuBois Farms.

Image credits

Photography and artwork
1: iStockphoto/Thinkstock; 2 (chicks tl): cornelia_anghel/Fotolia; 2 (chick tr): nicolesy/iStockphoto; 2 (computer monitor): skodonnell/iStockphoto; 2 (tickets): laurent gendre/Fotolia; 2 (duck): Lindamstyle/Dreamstime; 2 (chicken): Giuseppe Lancia/Dreamstime; 2 (fence, used throughout): Levkr/Dreamstime; 2 (alpacas): iStockphoto/Thinkstock; 3 (arrows): pagadesign/iStockphoto; 4 (piglet): GlobalP/iStockphoto; 4–5 (inset grass background, used throughout): Satel22/Dreamstime; 4 (goat t): ksena32/Fotolia; 4 (standing lamb): JMichl/iStockphoto; 4 (sitting lamb): Hem/Thinkstock; 4 (sheep): iStockphoto/Thinkstock; 4 (bunny): Konstantin Yolshin/Shutterstock; 4 (goat b): ksena32/Fotolia; 4 (pony): Elena Titarenco/Dreamstime; 4 (cows): PerfectLazybones/Fo[...]; 4 (guinea pig): Vasily77/Dreamstime; 4 (signpost, used throughout): Photka/Dreamstime; 4 (icons l to r): Guilu/Dreamstime, Sergey Yakovlev/Dreamstime, Tribalium/Dreamstime, Roughcoll[...]; Dreamstime; 5 (map): Yin21205/Dreamstime; 5 (handwashing icon): Tribalium/Dreamstime; 5 (alpaca tl): James Brey/iStockphoto; 5 (ducklings): Isselee/Dreamstime, Cristian Baitg/iStockph[...]; jarenwicklund/iStockphoto; 5 (white duck): Vasyl Helevachuk/Dreamstime; 5 (pig): GlobalP/iStockphoto; 5 (chicken): Giuseppe Lancia/Dreamstime; 5 (chicks): Sunnybeach/iStockphoto; 5 (g[...]; pigs): Gerritgr/Fotolia; 5 (alpaca br): Marie-T/iStockphoto; 5 (duckling bl): Chepko/iStockphoto; 6–7 (sky, grass, used throughout): Tatyana Vychegzhanina/Dreamstime; 6 (goat cl): Isselee/Dreamstime; 7 (goat tl): GlobalP/iStockphoto; 7 (billy): Iakov Filimonov/Dreamstime; 7 (nanny): Andygaylor/Dreamstime; 7 (kid b): Snickerdoodle Photography/iStockphoto; 7 (gate b): Amandamhanna/Dreamstime; 7 (latch): Soundsnaps/Dreamstime; 6–7 (all others): Penny Lamprell/Scholastic Inc.; 8 (goat, hay): Martijn Mulder/Dreamstime; 8 (wood background): Pedro20[...]; Dreamstime; 8bl: Christian Jung/Dreamstime; 8bcl: Kulikova/Dreamstime; 8bcr: Ahmet Gündoan/Dreamstime; 8br: Peter Zijlstra/Dreamstime; 9 (goat l): Tanaway/Dreamstime; 9 (goat r, background): ACMPhoto/iStockphoto; 9 (hay b): Kelpfish/Dreamstime; 9 (hand icon, used throughout): Samuvel/Dreamstime; 9 (inset): Poco_bw/Dreamstime; 9 (sheep icon): Guilu/Dreams[...]; 9 (grass below signpost, used throughout): Skalapendra/Dreamstime; 9 (lamb): GlobalP/iStockphoto; 10: GoodOlga/iStockphoto; 11tc: Grigorios Moraitis/iStockphoto; 11 (inset): Robert Wisdom/Dreamstime; 11 (fleece): esemelwe/iStockphoto; 11cl: shirhan/iStockphoto; 11 (sweater): BVDC/iStockphoto; 11 (bunny icon): Roughcollie/Dreamstime; 11 (bunny): Isselee/Dreams[...]; 12 (white bunny tl): Duncan Noakes/Dreamstime; 12 (mother, baby tl): Isselee/Dreamstime; 12–13 (red wood b): Tombaky/Dreamstime; 12–13 (straw b): Kelpfish/Dreamstime; 12 (large brow[...]; bunny): GlobalP/iStockphoto; 12 (inset): Penny Lamprell/Scholastic Inc.; 12–13 (leaping bunny): George Caswell/Getty Images; 13 (alpaca icon): Lantapix/Dreamstime; 13 (brown bunny r): Rubberball/Mike Kemp/Getty Images; 14: Alison Williams/Dreamstime; 15 (sky): Elena Elisseeva/Dreamstime; 15tl: Zoom-zoom/Fotolia; 15 (map): Adamgibson/Dreamstime; 15 (landscape): jeantrekkeur/Fotolia; 15 (alpaca herd): Christian Larue/Fotolia; 15 (inset): Levranii/Dreamstime; 15 (duck icon): Sergey Yakovlev/Dreamstime; 15 (ducklings): Stefan Andronache[...]; Dreamstime; 16 (ducklings, duck tl): Thierry Vialard/Dreamstime, GlobalP/iStockphoto, Danil Chepko/Dreamstime; 16 (inset): Penny Lamprell/Scholastic Inc.; 16 (main duckling): Photowitch/Dreamstime; 16–17 (green reeds): Tommason/Dreamstime; 16–17 (water): Melissa King/Dreamstime; 17 (l ducklings t to b): vusta/iStockphoto, Studio-Annika/iStockphoto, GlobalP/iStockp[...]; JodiJacobson/iStockphoto, Anatolii/Fotolia; 17 (white ducks): Penny Lamprell/Scholastic Inc.; 17 (pond tr): Leelloo/Dreamstime; 17 (duckling tr): Olga Yastremska/Dreamstime; 17 (pig icon): Batagaja/Dreamstime; 17 (pig): Miiicha/iStockphoto; 18–19 (straw background, sty): Edward Westmacott/iStockphoto; 18 (pigs): janecat/iStockphoto; 19 (inset t): Image_Source_/iStockph[...]; 19 (pig family): Susan Sheldon/Dreamstime; 19 (straw c): Nito100/Dreamstime; 19 (red wood): Tombaky/Dreamstime; 19 (green wood): nataliazakharova/Fotolia; 19 (guinea pig l): Alptraum/Dreamstime; 19 (guinea pig c): Simone Van Der Berg/Dreamstime; 19 (guinea pig r): GlobalP/iStockphoto; 19 (inset b): Penny Lamprell/Scholastic Inc.; 20–21 (main image): Eduard Kyslynsk[...]; Dreamstime; 20 (mud splatters): Roberto Pirola/Dreamstime; 20 (sunscreen): ARSELA/iStockphoto; 21tl: Michael Sheehan/Dreamstime; 21br: Stu Porter/Dreamstime; 21tcr: jlandrow/iStockphoto; 21tr: gennaro coretti/Fotolia; 21 (chicken): Sval77/Dreamstime; 21 (chicken icon): Tribalium/Dreamstime; 22 (background): nataliazakharova/Fotolia; 22 (hen, nest): thieury/Shutterstock; 22 (quail egg): Lepas/Dreamstime; 22 (quail): Boobathy/Dreamstime; 22 (robin egg): Linda Yolanda/iStockphoto; 22 (robin): Pperegrin/Dreamstime; 22 (chicken egg): Chris Leachman/Dreamstime; 22 (chicken): Anatolii/Fotolia; 22 (duck egg): Kooslin/Dreamstime; 22 (duck): Linda Steward/iStockphoto; 23 (chicken): Giuseppe Lancia/Dreamstime; 23 (chick): Photowitch/Dreamstime; 23 (egg tr): Chris Leachman/Dreamstime; 23 (hatching chick, egg): Photowitch/Dreamstime; 23 (penguin egg, penguin): Isselee/Dreamstime; 23 (goose egg): Vasy[...]; Helevachuk/Dreamstime; 23 (goose): Sean Nel/Dreamstime; 23 (emu egg): dovate/iStockphoto; 23 (emu): GlobalP/iStockphoto; 23 (ostrich egg): ayala_studio/iStockphoto; 23 (ostrich): vbli[...]; iStockphoto; 24 (inset): SKLA/iStockphoto; 24 (chicken tr): panbazil/Shutterstock; 24–25 (roof): Penny Lamprell/Scholastic Inc.; 24–25 (green wood): nataliazakharova/Fotolia; 24 (gray wood): enviromantic/iStockphoto; 24–25 (brown wood): Dreamstimepoint/Dreamstime; 24bc: panbazil/Shutterstock; 24br: Isselee/Dreamstime; 25 (cow icon): Darrenw/Dreamstime; 25 (calf): JMich[...]; iStockphoto; 25 (chicken tl, chick): panbazil/Shutterstock; 25bc: Ammit Jack/Shutterstock; 25br: Margojh/Dreamstime; 26–27 (background): Pedro2009/Dreamstim[...]; 26 (inset): emholk/iStockphoto; 26–27 (main): Dr. Ajay Kumar Singh/Dreamstime; 27 (inset): Drs. Cathe and Nick Tallarico; 27 (shed): patty_c/iStockphoto; 27 (Little Nicky): Drs. Cathe and Ni[...]; Tallarico; 27 (pony icon): Roughcollie/Dreamstime; 28–29 (bushes, white fence): Johannesk/Dreamstime; 28–29 (main image): Elena Titarenco/Dreamstime; 28 (gate b): jorgesa/iStockphoto; (gray wood): enviromantic/iStockphoto; 29 (ride a pony): Elena Titarenco/Dreamstime; 29 (bunny): Pavla Zakova/Dreamstime; 29 (chick): hartcreations/iStockphoto; 29 (goat): xiao-ming/iStockphoto; 29 (piglet): SchulteProductions/iStockphoto; 30–31 (main image): Tanaway/Dreamstime; 31 (handwashing icon): Tribalium/Dreamstime; 31 (duckling): Art_man/Fotolia; 31 (bunnies): camellias/Fotolia; 32 (meadow): Monika3stepsahead/Dreamstime; 32 (duckling): jarenwicklund/iStockphoto; 32 (pig): GlobalP/iStockphoto; all others: Scholastic Inc.

Cover
Front cover: (sheep icon) Oorka/Dreamstime; (rooster icon) Talisalex/Dreamstime; (goat icon) Oorka/Dreamstime; (bunny icon) Ashestos/Dreamstime; (donkey icon) Oorka/Dreamstime; (duck icon) Lantapix/Dreamstime; (trees) Nikada/iStockphoto; (bl) Belkin & Co/Fotolia; (br) Farinoza/Fotolia; (grass) narvikk/iStockphoto. Back cover: (tr) GlobalP/iStockphoto; (computer monitor) Manaemedia/Dreamstime. Inside front cover: (ducks) Thomas Seybold/iStockphoto; (br) Yakovliev/iStockphoto.